185172

EXTREME SPORTS

BMX FREESTYLE

BY THOMAS K. ADAMSON

EPIC

BELLWETHER MEDIA • MINNEAPOLIS, MN

EPIC BOOKS are no ordinary books. They burst with intense action, high-speed heroics, and shadows of the unknown. Are you ready for an Epic adventure?

This edition first published in 2016 by Bellwether Media, Inc.

No part of this publication may be reproduced in whole or in part without written permission of the publisher. For information regarding permission, write to Bellwether Media, Inc., Attention: Permissions Department, 5357 Penn Avenue South, Minneapolis, MN 55419.

Library of Congress Cataloging-in-Publication Data

Adamson, Thomas K., 1970-
  BMX Freestyle / by Thomas K. Adamson.
     pages cm. – (Epic: Extreme Sports)
  Summary: "Engaging images accompany information about BMX freestyle. The combination of high-interest subject matter and light text is intended for students in grades 2 through 7"– Provided by publisher.
  Audience: Ages 7 to 12
  Includes bibliographical references and index.
  ISBN 978-1-62617-273-9 (hardcover: alk. paper)
  1. BMX freestyle (Stunt cycling)–Juvenile literature. 2. Extreme sports–Juvenile literature. 3. ESPN X-Games–Juvenile literature. I. Title.
  GV1049.3.A326 2016
  796.6'22–dc23
                         2015005968

Printed in the United States of America, North Mankato, MN.

TABLE OF CONTENTS

WARNING
The tricks shown in this book are performed by professionals. Always wear a helmet and other safety gear when you are on a bike.

VERT VICTORY

Jamie Bestwick drops in the halfpipe. He picks up speed on his BMX bike. Bestwick flies above the halfpipe's coping. He spins and flips for his first **trick**. He lands with ease.

Bestwick does more tricks perfectly. Near the end of his **run**, he lands a front flip flair. He then completes three more hard tricks to finish his run. Bestwick wins 2014 X Games BMX Vert gold!

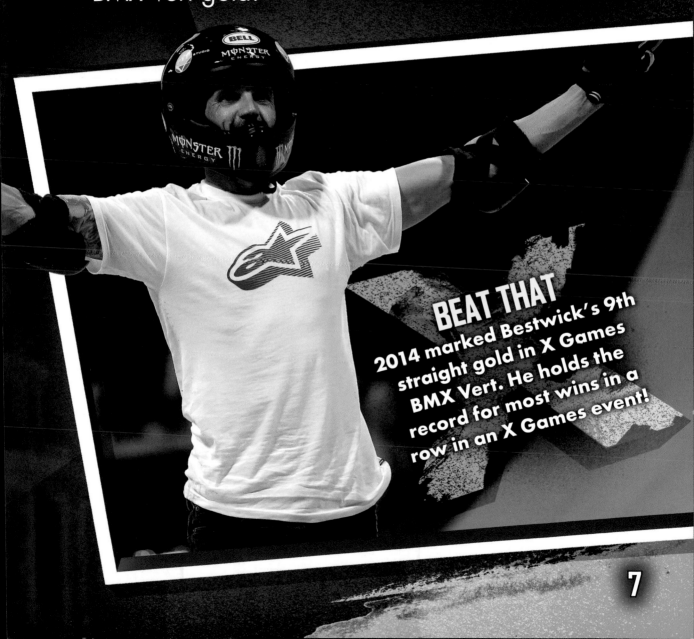

BEAT THAT

2014 marked Bestwick's 9th straight gold in X Games BMX Vert. He holds the record for most wins in a row in an X Games event!

BMX FREESTYLE

In BMX freestyle, riders do tricks with small, **agile** bikes. Some freestyle riders show off their moves high above a halfpipe. Others pull tricks on objects found on the street.

B-M-X
BMX is short for bicycle motocross.

Freestyle BMX riders also ride on dirt tracks. They fly off of big ramps. Some freestyle riders do not use jumps. Flatland BMX bikers need a lot of balance to do their **stunts**.

BMX FREESTYLE TERMS

big air—a freestyle event in which riders drop down a huge launch ramp and jump across a gap

coping—the top edge of a halfpipe

dirt track—a freestyle event on a winding dirt track with ramps and jumps

drop in—to begin biking in a halfpipe

flatland—a freestyle event in which riders do tricks on flat pavement with no obstacles

front flip flair—a flip with a 180-degree turn

halfpipe—a set of ramps that look like the bottom half of a pipe

no-handed 900—two and a half spins in the air during which the rider lets go of the handlebars

park—a freestyle event in what looks like an empty swimming pool

street—a freestyle event on a course using objects that might be found on the street

vert—a freestyle event that uses a halfpipe

BMX BEGINNINGS

In the 1960s and 1970s, kids wanted to be like motorcycle riders. They raced their bikes on dirt tracks. They often did tricks during these races.

IN THE MOVIES
The 1971 movie *On Any Sunday* opened with kids racing bicycles on a dirt track. The scene helped make BMX popular.

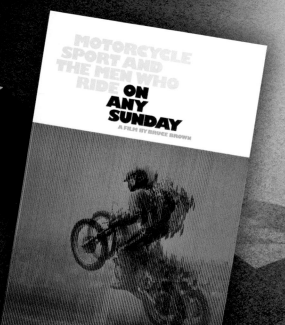

MOTORCYCLE SPORT AND THE MEN WHO RIDE ON ANY SUNDAY
A FILM BY BRUCE BROWN

Some BMX riders moved to empty pools and skate parks. They used bigger jumps and other **obstacles** for their tricks. The sport changed and grew with each new idea.

BMX GEAR

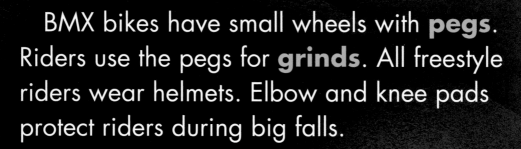

BMX bikes have small wheels with **pegs**. Riders use the pegs for **grinds**. All freestyle riders wear helmets. Elbow and knee pads protect riders during big falls.

GO FOR A SPIN
Freestyle BMX bikes only have a brake on the front wheel. A brake on the rear wheel would get tangled during tricks.

THE COMPETITION

The 2014 X Games had five BMX freestyle events. Riders competed in Vert, Street, Park, and Dirt competitions. Some even tried out BMX Big Air.

BMX Big Air

EVENT SCORING

Judges give riders a score out of 100 points for each run. They look for difficult and new tricks.

BMX Vert

GAMES AUSTIN

GAMES ★ AUSTIN

In each event, BMX freestyle riders get two, three, or four runs. Only the best run counts. That way, riders can take a chance on a really hard trick. If they fall, they can still win on another run.

INNOVATOR OF THE SPORT

name: **Mat Hoffman**
birthdate: **January 9, 1972**
hometown: **Oklahoma City, Oklahoma**
innovations: **Invented more than 100 tricks and was the first rider to land a no-handed 900**

GLOSSARY

agile—able to move quickly and easily

grinds—tricks in which the rider slides the bike's pegs or frame along an object

obstacles—objects that BMX riders use for tricks

pegs—metal bars that stick out from a bike's wheel; BMX riders use pegs to grind.

run—a turn at competing in an event

stunts—acts that show great skill or daring

trick—a specific move in a BMX freestyle event

TO LEARN MORE

AT THE LIBRARY

Cain, Patrick G. *BMX Vert*. Minneapolis, Minn.: Lerner Publications, 2013.

Cohn, Jessica. *BMX*. New York, N.Y.: Gareth Stevens Pub., 2013.

Stuckey, Rachel. *Ride It BMX*. New York, N.Y.: Crabtree Pub., 2012.

ON THE WEB

Learning more about BMX freestyle is as easy as 1, 2, 3.

1. Go to www.factsurfer.com.

2. Enter "BMX freestyle" into the search box.

3. Click the "Surf" button and you will see a list of related web sites.

With factsurfer.com, finding more information is just a click away.

INDEX

The images in this book are reproduced through the courtesy of: homydesign, front cover, p. 16; Rustin Gudim/ Zuma Press, pp. 4-5; Ezra Shaw/ Getty Images, pp. 6, 7, 18-19; Dmitry Elagin, p. 8; Joe Maher/ WENN/ Newscom, p. 9; Dan Wozniak/ Zuma Press, p. 10; Zuma Press/ Alamy, p. 11; Everett Collection/ Alamy, p. 12; NCJ Mirrorpix/ Newscom, pp. 12-13; ITV/ Rex/ Newscom, p. 14; Photofusion/ Getty Images, p. 15; Duomo/ Corbis, p. 17; Christian Pondella/ Getty Images, p. 19; David R. Rico/ Demotix/ Corbis, p. 20; Tony Donaldson/ Icon SMI/ Newscom, p. 21; Bo Bridges/ Corbis, p. 21 (top).